Beginnings

Until the Romans o
ning of the first mille......
across the River Cam, only an ancient ford near to where Magdalene College now stands; this crossing is where the Romans chose to build their bridge.

The Romans established a military headquarters on the high ground to the north-west of the river, which was a staging post on the way north to York. The headquarters of Cambridgeshire County Council now stands on this site.

The Roman bridge carried a road across the river leading into the centre of a developing commercial town, towards where the Round Church now stands. There the road split into an arm that led south-east to Colchester, their principal garrison town in eastern England, and another south-westerly to London, their principal port and link to Gaul and the rest of their empire in mainland Europe.

Nothing remains above ground of the few hundred years that the Romans were in Cambridge. However, it is worth remembering that while you follow this walk, beneath your feet is not only the modern tarmac, but the medieval High Street, which in turn sits atop the Roman road to London. This road, in true Roman style, leads due south to its destination with hardly a bend.

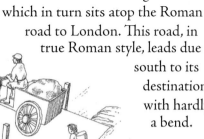

Section One - Magdalene Street

Let us begin our walk near the bridge in Magdalene Street. Cambridge University is a collegiate university of 31 independent colleges and a central University administration, you will pass nine of the oldest Colleges during this walk.

Magdalene College   *a*

The college was originally founded in 1428 as a monastery for monks studying at the University; it suffered from King Henry VIII's dissolution of the monasteries in 1539, but in 1542 the Lord Chancellor, Lord Audley of Walden, was given permission by Henry to re-found it under a new dedication to St Mary Magdalene.

At this time the name was written and pronounced 'Maudleyn', which contains Lord Audley's name, a piece of vanity that survives in the current pronunciation of 'Maudlyn'.

Magdalene college coat of arms

Magdalene's best-known alumnus is Samuel Pepys (1633-1703), a cadet member of the family that became the Earls of Cottenham, named after a Cambridgeshire village. He studied at Magdalene from 1650 to 1654, and bequeathed his college the six manuscript volumes of his famous diary, which is stored in a special 'Pepys Building' with all the three thousand volumes of his private library. They can be viewed by the general public at certain times, which are obtainable from the Porters' Lodge.

Magdalene Street

A roof with a double pitch in its slope is called a Mansard roof. Its shape allows more height in the attic room. The window poking through the roof is termed a Dormer.

If you look at a house close to the bridge you will discover that the window really does look like this.
Movement in this old timber-framed building has caused the 19th century window to distort.

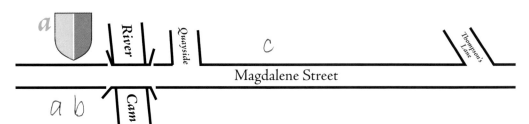

Magdalene Street

Magdalene College from Quayside

As you walk across the bridge towards the city centre down to your left is Quayside. Originally developed by the Vikings as a quay in the late 9th century, to increase trade, it is now used to hire punts out - be careful though, punting is not as easy as it looks!

Medieval buildings, with 19th century fronts

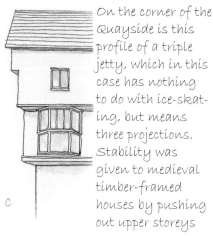

On the corner of the Quayside is this profile of a triple jetty, which in this case has nothing to do with ice-skating, but means three projections. Stability was given to medieval timber-framed houses by pushing out upper storeys

c

d

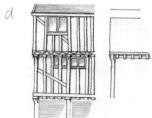

Almost all of the timber framing in Bridge House is genuine 16th century. It has a double jetty, and the horizontal bressemers are carved with a course, or line, of oak leaves.

On the left side of Bridge Street is a range of 16th century buildings, which were due for demolition and re-development in the 1970s, until David Peace, a planning officer, ensured that the front ranges of the old buildings were saved by only allowing the rear of the buildings to be developed. One of these houses, timber-framed and double-jettied, Bridge House, is a striking example of Tudor domestic architecture. Notice the upper floors, supported by horizontal bressemers placed on projecting joists. Most of the timbers of all the houses here are the original 16th to 17th century work and are as good now as when they were first put up 500 years ago, reflecting the superb workmanship and quality of materials in Tudor times.

We now reach the Round Church.

Portugal Place

d

Bridge Street

St. Joh

Sidney

Section Two - St.John's Street

The Church of the Holy Sepulchre *b*

Built from 1130 and associated with crusad-
ing Knights. Their orders were formed to guard
the Holy Land and protect the Holy Sepulchre
in Jerusalem, where Christ was reputed to have
been buried. The Round Church is one of the five
round churches built in the Romanesque Norman
style still remaining in England. The building is
now used as a brass-rubbing centre.

The Church of the
Holy Sepulchre

At this point we turn right into St John's Street.

St John's Street (Nos. 12 – 16)

These are medieval houses, partly
remodelled in the 16th and
17th centuries, but principally
in the 19th century, when they
were first turned into shops.

e

*We could not resist asking
you to look up at the
roof line across the
road from St John's
college. A 19th
century chimney
stack with each
chimney pot serv-
ing at least one fireplace.*

St John's College *c*

The first building on the right side of St John's
Street, which was called the High Street in
medieval times, is St. John's College. It was
founded in 1511 by Lady Margaret of Beaufort,
Countess of Richmond and Derby, daughter of
John Beaufort, Duke of Somerset. Margaret
married, as her second of four husbands, Edmund
Tudor, the illegitimate son of Owen Tudor and
Henry V's widow, Katharine of France. Their son,
Henry, became the first Tudor monarch, Henry
VII (1485). The college was built on the original
mediaeval site of the hospital of St John.

The heraldic sculpture over *f*
*the main gate to
St John's College
shows the Coat
of Arms of Lady
Margaret Beaufort.
The strange
animals, acting as supporters,
are a concoction of antelope
bodies, goats' heads and
elephants' tails. They
are called Yales.*

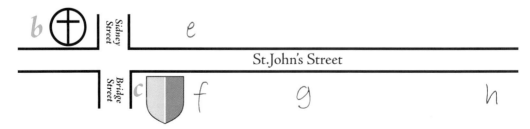

b *Sidney Street* *e*

St.John's Street

Bridge Street *c* *f* *g* *h*

g

The walls of the three older courts of St John's reveal a history of English brickwork through the 15th to the 17th centuries. The street view shows the dark blue ends of high-fired bricks creating a pattern. These examples of ways of making horizontal courses of bricks shows two ways of laying them. One has alternating rows of stretchers (the sides) and headers (the ends); called English bond. The other shows headers and stretchers alternating along each course; called Flemish bond.

h

This Oriel window is close to Trinity College's great gate, there are lots of them on our route. An Oriel is a projecting bay window that does not continuously extend down to the ground. Its style is a 19th century version of Medieval Gothic.

The present Chapel, by Sir George Gilbert Scott, the Gothicist, built 1863-69, replaced an older one, the foundations of which can still be seen. The buildings in red brick were finished in 1516 and later restored, rather than replaced. The poet, William Wordsworth, was a student in 1770, and his brother, Christopher, became Master of Trinity College (1820-1841).

St John's Chapel

d

The Old Divinity Schools
These were built on the left side of St John's Street by the architect Basil Champneys. The Schools were built in 1877 in the Gothic style during the peak of the High Victorian Gothic period. Champneys later became one of the

Old Divinity Schools

pioneers of the much lighter Queen Anne style of architecture which he used when building Newnham College, also in Cambridge.

All Saints' Garden and Passage   e
In medieval times, when St John's Street was part of the Cambridge High Street, All Saints' Church, formerly known as All Hallows, dating back to the 11th century, projected into the already narrow street and in 1865 it was demolished to widen the road. The present garden was the graveyard.

At this point St John's Street becomes Trinity Street.

d   All Saints' Passage   e   All Saints' Passage
St.John's Street   Trinity Street

Section Three - Trinity Street

The Post Office
This building has an early 20th century shop front. The brickwork and windows above are early 18th century. The cornice at the eaves is wooden, which dates the building to very early 18th century, when an ordinance, for safety reasons, determined that all cornices should be of brick or stone.

Trinity College *f*
Founded by Henry VIII in 1546, this building replaced the existing teaching institutions that covered the area between St John's and Garret Hostel Lane, which is the pathway between Trinity College and Trinity Hall. The original gatehouse was remodelled to produce the existing

Trinity Street Post Office, apart from its shop front, has a Georgian appearance. This drawing shows a late-18th century sash window, which rises up and down on cords, or sashes. Each lintel is decorated with a masque. Prominent corner stones or bricks are called 'quoins' (pronounced in English as 'kwoyns')

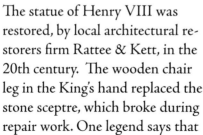

Great Gate.
The statue of Henry VIII was restored, by local architectural restorers firm Rattee & Kett, in the 20th century. The wooden chair leg in the King's hand replaced the stone sceptre, which broke during repair work. One legend says that the chair leg is reputed to have been taken from a chair in the Porter's Lodge by one of the porters. The large, impressive chapel is in Perpendicular style, seen in the predominating vertical elements of its tracery and panelling. Two notable alumni were Lord Byron, who came up in 1805 with his pet bear, and Sir Isaac Newton, the father of modern science, here between 1669 and 1701.

Trinity college
'Great Gate'

St.John's Street

The Post Office along
to The Blue Boar

Triple-jettied to the triangular
gables. The present façade was
remodelled in the early 17th
century to 'hide' the older joists.
The decoration in the plaster-
work is called pargeting.

The projecting porch-like arched
cover is termed a hood-mould,
aimed at giving protection from
the rain when waiting to climb
into a horse-drawn coach. This
shape was
fashionable
in the late
17th and
early 18th
centuries.

Heffer's Bookshop to Green Street

Back on the left side of the street, this world-
famous bookseller's stands on a totally modernised site, but an 18th century appearance is maintained in reddish brickwork and dressing around
elegant sash windows in upper storeys. Next door
is Heffer's Sound. This 17th century building has
vertical pilasters, Vetruvian scrolls and a two-
pitched Mansard roof, so-named after the French
architects, the Mansart brothers, who first used
this design in the 17th century.

The Blue Boar is a former early 19th century
coaching inn, the inside was completely refash-
ioned in the mid-20th century, but the 17th
century shell hood still sits over the entrance.

No.15 is an 18th century fronted house, which
now accommodates a 20th century coffee house.
Parts of the cellar reveal great 16th century
timbers.
No.14 is a timber-framed medieval house,
modernised in the early 17th century, was
formerly The Turk's Head inn, then Foster's Bank.
No.10 is on the corner of Green Street. This
building used to accommodate the 'Whim' café, a
favoured breakfast place of Prince Charles, Prince
of Wales when he was a Trinity undergraduate
in the 1960s. All the waitresses had to be public-
school educated and could only talk to the
customers if they were introduced by one of
the two old sisters who owned the place.

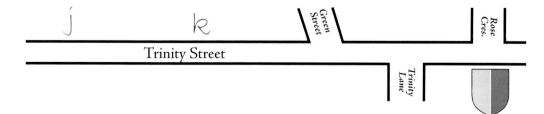

Trinity Street

Section Four - Trinity Street

Trinity Lane is on the opposite side of Trinity Street i.e. the right side, and runs between Trinity and Gonville & Caius Colleges.

Gonville and Caius College *g*

Founded as Gonville Hall in 1348 by Edmund Gonville, a priest, who was vicar of several East Anglian parishes. He used the tithes from his livings to fund the building of his college but died before it was built. His bishop, Bishop Bateman, founder of nearby Trinity Hall, then finished it. Gonville had acquired land where Corpus Christi now stands (see later), but Bateman arranged an exchange with the Guilds that owned the land where Gonville & Caius now stands.

Gonville Hall only just survived over the next two centuries, until, John Keys of Norwich, a rich physician to the Tudor monarchs Edward VI and Queen Mary, refounded it as a College in 1557. He Latinized his name to Caius (still pronounced Keys) by which name the College is generally known. Caius also commissioned the three gates for which Gonville and Caius College is well known named Humility, Virtue and Honour, built in an Italianate Renaissance style. The gate of Honour is used by undergraduates on their way to the Senate House for graduation. Alfred Waterhouse completely rebuilt Tree Court, which adjoins Trinity Street, in French Chateau style between 1868 and 1870.

If you look up at the corner of Trinity Lane, the street name, the modern street lamp and the security cameras have been removed from this drawing because we want you to note the different coloured bricks. It saved the owner money to restrict the more expensive bricks to the façade and use the cheaper, local ones for the side.

The Waterhouse Tower
Gonville & Caius College
(seen from Kings College Chapel)

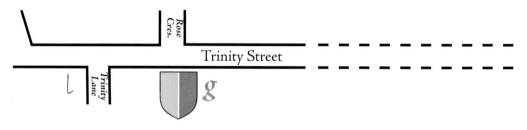

Rose Cres.

Trinity Street

Trinity Lane   *g*

St Michael's Church

St Michael's Church *h*

This church, opposite Gonville and Caius College, was built in the first half of the 14th century and granted by the Bishop of Ely, John Hotham, to Hervey de Stanton as the parish collegiate church of Michaelhouse in 1324. Unusually for the time the nave is much smaller than the choir, a design later used by many collegiate churchs.

In 2002/3, the interior was remodelled into a multi-purpose building suitable for use as a gallery, small concert hall, café and for occasional church services.

No.3 is a 16th century timber-framed building with window-glazing bars, wooden cornice, mansard roof, two dormer windows and parapet.

Nos.2 & 1 Cambridge University Press bookshop, formerly Bowes & Bowes, has a claim to be the oldest bookshop site in the country, having sold books there since 1581. The building consists of two medieval houses, cased in 18th century brick with 19th century windows, placed over medieval casements and joined to make one building.

m

Just before the corner with St. Mary's Street is a doctors' surgery and the sash windows show large panes of glass, of a size first shown at the Great Exhibition of 1851, and slight projections at the lower ends of the vertical edges, called horns. Horns were invented about 1880 to strengthen the pinned joint with the lower rail. The top floor windows with thick glazing bars and no horns are early 18th century.

n The upper windows of the Cambridge University Press bookshop are stunningly elegant examples of early 19th century design.
The simple cast-iron guards were to contain window boxes resting on the sills.

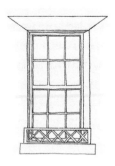

h ⊞ *m*   *n*   St. Mary's Street

Trinity Street

Senate House Passage

Section Five - King's Parade I

Great St. Mary's Church   *i*

Dominating the Market Square with its face on King's Parade stands the University Church, Great St Mary's, which was begun at the end of the 12th century, finished in 1205 and remodelled in the 15th century. The window tracery pattern is in Perpendicular style. The West Tower was built between 1491 and 1550. The views over the City from the top of this tower, which the public can climb for a small fee, are fantastic. The bells ring out the quarters, increasing in length as they get to the hour. Avoid being on the twister or spiral staircase when they ring noon!

Great St. Mary's Church

o   One of the pinnacles crowning the roof of Great St Mary's church. The projecting leafy bud-like shapes extending up the corner edges of the tiny spires are called sprockets.

Senate House   *j*

Situated on the west side of King's Parade, opposite Great St Mary's, is the official centre of Cambridge University, one of the finest examples of English 18th century architecture. Here successful undergraduates receive their degrees from the Vice-Chancellor in a ceremony where Latin is still used today. The architect was James Gibbs, who also built St Martin-in-the-Fields in Trafalgar Square, London. Building took place from 1722-1730, and was extended by James Essex in 1730.

p   The Senate House displays a catalogue of classical 18th century designs. Our drawing focuses on a corner that shows the balcony, with its balusters, the entablature, which is a layered series of a variety of decorative features, resting on the elaborately carved capital of a column.

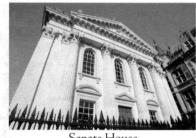

Senate House

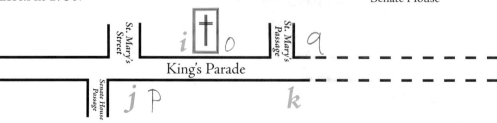

The Old Schools *k*

These lie at right angles to the end of Senate House behind the Senate House Green. What one sees from the road is a screen built by the architect Stephen Wright in 1754 in front of medieval buildings that provide the administrative centre for the University. A glimpse of the earlier Gothic building can be seen from halfway down Senate House Passage opposite Caius' Gate of Honour. The Old Schools were also the original site for the now famous Cambridge University Library, one of the six legal deposit libraries in the British Isles.

One very small building displaying 17th century 'modernisations' in its dormer, square-bay window and small rain-hood over the door, reveals an original size and proportion that dates back to the 15th century, when the Town Burgesses allocated a building plot to the first owner.

St Mary's Passage

Continuing our walk along the left side of King's Parade, we pass St Mary's Passage, bordering the small churchyard to the south of Great St Mary's Church and leading to the Market Place. It contains a line of 16th century houses, remodelled in the 18th and 19th century.

No. 1 - St Mary's Passage

Auntie's Tea Shop. This is a good place to take a cup of tea or coffee, sitting at one of the tables outside, or if the weather drives you indoors, looking out of the plate-glass window Look up at the third floor and you will see three windows, of which only the central one is real, the other two are false, having been cut into a parapet that was raised on each side of the dormer window to make this look a more substantial town house. All becomes clear, when viewed from Great St Mary's Tower.

Section Six - King's Parade II

No. 22 - Ryder & Amies

This timber-framed, medieval building, encased in red brick in the 18th
century, is the principal university shop
in Cambridge, having purveyed university wear,
sports-clothes, badges, academical dress, etc., for
over two centuries. If varsity sport is one of your
interests, information on sports fixtures and team
lists can be seen in their window. They also,
unusually, accept most currencies.

The stylish letter-forms
along the facias on the angled
sides of this shop are in the
Arts and Crafts style that was
fashionable from 1856 until
about 1925.

Before the building of King's College (1441) the
road which now forms King's Parade was narrow
with rows of tall houses on both sides. Much of
the west side was demolished by King Henry VI
down as far as the river in order to build his
college. He removed most of the busy commercial,
dock area along the River Cam, no trace of which
remains.

A drawing
of a fragment
of the King's Parade roof line to
remind you that there is much
to discover and wonder at above
a street's façade.

The range of buildings that remain on
the left side of King's Parade as far as
Bene't (short for St Benedict) Street
are medieval timber-framed houses,
remodelled largely in the 18th and
19th centuries and transformed into
shops. Many of them are faced with
the traditional Cambridgeshire white
bricks. The door of No. 2 with
its decorative casing is a late 18th
century gem.

One of a fine selec-
tion of door-casings
along King's Parade.
Late 18th century, the
columns supporting
the triangular-shaped
pediment have large
voluted brackets

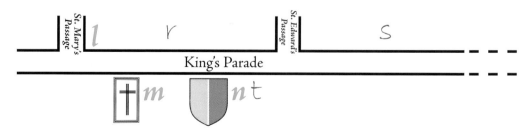

Kings College chapel

The distinctive
mitre-like shape of
the pinnacles
atop King's
College Chapel,
made in
the final
pinnacle
shape of the
Late-Perpen-
dicular Gothic style before
England's break with what
became the Catholic Church.

King's College Chapel   *m*

Pause here and look across at one of the marvels of English Architecture, King's College Chapel. Possibly the most famous building in Cambridge it was designed by Henry VI in 1448. The building was continued by the next four Kings, Edward IV, Richard III, Henry VII, and finished about 1515 by his son, Henry VIII, all of whom, over a period of seventy years, followed the outline laid down by Henry VI. Inside the magnificent fan vaulted ceiling was completed between 1512-15 by master mason John Wastell. It is one of Europe's finest late medieval buildings and home to the world-famous Choir. Try to make time to look inside.

King's College   *n*

Founded in 1441 by Henry VI, who laid the foundation stone himself. .The College itself is hidden behind the stone screen and its pinnacled entrance lodge, in Gothic revival style, designed by William Wilkins in 1829. Wilkins also designed the National Gallery in London.
The writer EM Forster was a life long occupant of rooms in the college.

St Edward's Passage

Opposite King's Chapel this alleyway between the shops leads east to the tiny church of St Edward the Martyr, King of England 975-978 and murdered by retainers of his jealous half-brother, Ethelred, who then became King.
Opposite the church is the Arts Theatre, founded in 1935 by John Maynard Keynes, the great 20th century economist of King's College, as a gift to his Russian ballerina wife, Lydia Lopokova.

St Edward's Passage

Section Seven - King's Parade III

No. 10 - Bene't Street, Natwest Bank

This heavy Victorian building, faced with unnec-
essary, false buttresses, leads along Bene't Street to
a side entrance to Corpus Christi College and the
oldest building in Cambridge, the Saxon tower of
St Bene't's church.

No. 10

St Bene't's Church and The Eagle

St Bene't's Church tower was built in 1030, in the
reign of King Canute, and is a rare example of one
of the very few stone Saxon buildings in East
Anglia, a stoneless area. The Saxons normally
built in wood. The tower has the long and short
quoins (corner stones), typical of Anglo-Saxon
buildings. The remainder of the church came
much later. In the fourteenth century the church
was a meeting place for some of the Cambridge
Guilds, two of which went on to found Corpus
Christi College. The church still has strong links
with the college.

St Bene't's
Church

Almost opposite St Bene't's is the ancient coaching inn, The Eagle. During World War Two the
pub was a favourite haunt of American airmen,

The Eagle Pub

the RAF bar at the back of the
pub has writing burnt into the
ceiling dating from that era. It
was also the favourite pub of
Francis Crick and James Watson,
who, in 1953, announced their
discovery of DNA to everybody
in the bar.

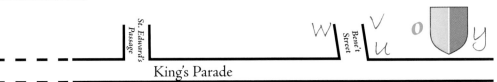

King's Parade

St. Edward's Passage

Bene't Street

St.Catharine's College

The 20th century Keynes build-ing of King's College links the 19th century  Gothic Revival with the 18th century of St Catherine's. Obviously modern, yet its proportions and the vertical feel of its simple design do not intrude, and many people do not even give it a second glance.

Corpus Christi College

The street range of Corpus Christi is 19th century and designed by William Wilkins, who designed the Screen of King's across the road. It has a moulded string-course along this front with decorative features placed along it. Hopefully the three masques that I have illustrated above may be identified.

We now leave King's Parade and the street reverts to its old name of Trumpington Street until it leaves the city and becomes Trumpington Road. The range of buildings skirting the left side of Trumpington Street was built by William Wilkins, the man who designed the King's College screen, in 1823.

Corpus Christi College

From the corner of Bene't Street it is a few steps past the 19th century houses built on the site of medieval houses to Corpus Christi College, whose best-known alumnus is the playwright Chris-topher Marlowe, who came up to Cambridge in 1580 from King's School, Canterbury, became a rival of Shakespeare, and is reputed by some to be the author of Shakespeare's plays.

Founded in 1352, Corpus Christi is the only medieval Cambridge College that was not founded by an individual, but by two Cambridge Guilds, an association of like-minded merchants engaged in similar trades. The Guild of Corpus Christi along with the Guild of the Virgin Mary appropriated St Bene't's Church and built their college on its land.

The College Library contains the most important extant copy of the Anglo-Saxon Chronicle and many other unique Anglo-Saxon documents, all donated by Archbishop Matthew Parker, who became a Fellow of Corpus in 1527 and a leading Protestant divine. These can be viewed by the public, the visiting times are available from the Porters' Lodge.

Section Eight - King's Parade to Trumpington

St Catharine's College   *p*

St Catharine's College was founded by the third Provost of King's College, Dr. Robert Wodelarke, in 1473, and named after the legendary Christian martyr who was tortured by being spun on a spiked wheel, which exploded and released her. The Catharine Wheel firework was named after her, and the wheel appears in the college crest, featured above the college gates. Everything we see today was added in the 17th and 18th centuries after the demolition of existing buildings.

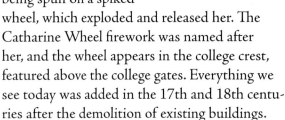

The St Catharine's drawing shows a suppressed or basket arch of the late 17th century decorated with teeth-like dentils and supported by curly Ionic capitals. An oval window with a stone surround or architrave is placed within its wall. The final fashionable feature of this Restoration period is a range of large dormer windows with alternating triangular or segmented pediments.

Thomas Hobson, a sixteenth century Cambridge carrier, kept his horses in a yard where the 'Catz' College chapel now stands, not visible from the road. Hobson rented out horses for the day, and has left a memento to the English language. His clients could choose any horse, so long as it was the one that Hobson offered them, i.e. 'Hobson's Choice' was no choice at all.

The Catharine wheel crest

An old fashioned Lamp-post, with a rest bar for the Lamplighter's ladder, that dates back to the days of gas street lighting when the mantle had to be lit by hand.

St. Catharine's College - 'Catz'

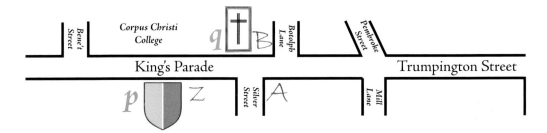

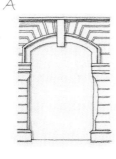

A

An architec-tural design, popular from the early 18th century, called Gibb's Surround. It could be built in either carved blocks of stone, brickwork with shaped edges, or rendered over in moulded stucco (plaster-ce-ment). In the same century a moulded ceramic material called Coade stone was created for such and similar work.

B

The tower of St Botolph's was rebuilt in the 15th century. Instead of the conventional pinnacles at each corner of the parapet it has sculp-tured figures of the Evangelists, all rather weatherworn. If you are blessed with good light then you will be amused to see the three symbolic beasts and one rather sad human.

Silver Street

Silver Street leads down to the river and the Mill Stream, where, before the building of King's College, boats and barges used to come upriver to collect corn and flour from the wharves be-side the mill, but where now stand two attractive refreshment stations, the 'Mill' and the 'Anchor' pubs. No-one knows how this street got its name. In medieval times, it was called Smalebriggestrate (Small Bridge Street as opposed to Great Bridge Street by Magadalene College). However, the name Silver Street was commonly used in medieval times.

St Botolph's Church   *9*

Opposite the entrance to Silver Street stands St Botolph's Church, this version of it being 14th century, but the name suggests a pre-Norman foundation, as St Botolph lived in the 7th century. Churches to St Botolph are regularly found close to the entrances of medieval town gates. The houses along the right side of the churchyard are built beside the medieval southern boundary of Cam-

bridge, the King's Ditch, now covered by Pem-broke Street as far as the Crowne Plaza Hotel, where it cuts at an angle across to Christ's College.

Section Nine - Trumpington Street I

Trumpington Gate *r*

The medieval Trumpington Gate would have stood approximately where the Cambridge University Press stands now. The gate was the entrance into Cambridge from the south, and was where Queen Elizabeth I entered Cambridge on horseback, making her only official visit to Cambridge, in 1564. The Queen was stopped here by the Mayor and Aldermen and given permission to enter the town. She attended a gathering of the University Senate, where all the business was done in Latin, and unexpectedly she was asked to reply to the Chancellor's speech of welcome. Without preparation or notes she delivered an extempore speech in the Latin tongue. Elizabeth, as well as being one of our best-ever monarchs, was a learned scholar and excellent linguist with a fluency in Greek, Latin, French and Italian.

C

Close to the entrance steps to the CUP-Pitt Building, that is often mistaken for a church or college building because of its 19th century Gothick appearance, are a pair of boot-scrapers. They are of elaborate design with cast-iron lions supporting mini fortified turrets.

Fitzbillies

Fitzbillies *s*

The 200 year-old cake shop is near the corner of Pembroke Street, which has a rounded corner, where the medieval end of the building had to be shaved off to accommodate the huge horse-drawn wagons that needed to turn this corner in the 18th and 19th centuries. Pembroke Street, adjoining Pembroke College, leads into Downing Street which is named after Sir George Downing, who left assets for the foundation of Downing College (at the far end of this road).

There are so many boot-scrapers in this part of Cambridge, but here is one last one tucked into the arched opening of this internationally famous baker and confectioner.

D

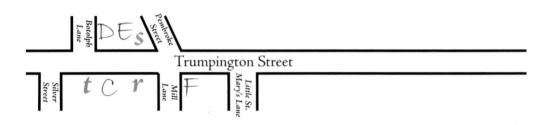

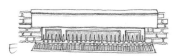

Across the road from the Pitt Building is this large sash-window which once gave light into a basement living area. It is now protected by iron-grating and a line of spikes.

Cambridge University Press

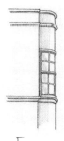

Narrow streets made the corners of buildings vulnerable to assault from passing wagons, and one method to avoid problems was to round off the sharp angles. This Mill Lane corner is very well done.

The first Sir George, his grandfather, had built Downing Street in London, where the official residences of the Prime Minister and Chancellor of the Exchequer are located (Nos. 10 & 11).

Along Pembroke Street, on the left, is Free School Lane. The Old Cavendish Laboratories are here, where the New Zealander, Ernest Rutherford, first split the atom and duly became the first Baron Rutherford of Nelson, New Zealand. This is also where Francis Crick and James Watson, the discoverers of DNA in 1953, worked in an old Nissen hut, now used as a bicycle shed!

Cambridge University Press   *t*

Across the road from Fitzbillies is a building with a large tower, which makes it look like a church, which it isn't. It is the headquarters of the world-renowned publisher, Cambridge University Press, the University printers and publisher of mainly academic works. CUP, as it is known, is the oldest printer and publisher in the world, and has operated continuously since 1584. Built in 1827 and called the Pitt Building, this building was funded by excess monies from a Trust formed to build a statue in honour of the Prime Minister, William Pitt the Younger, who died in 1806.

We are now outside medieval Cambridge, of which Trumpington Street and St Andrews Street were faubourgs, the Middle English word for suburb.

Section Ten - Trumpington Street II

Pembroke College   *u*

The college was founded in 1347 by Mary de St Pol, the Countess of Pembroke. Some of the land next to the college was acquired by Dr. Matthew Wren, Fellow of Pembroke, Master of the college on the other side of the road, Peterhouse, and Bishop of Ely. During the first Civil War (1642-1646), he was arrested and imprisoned in the Tower of London for eighteen years. He vowed to build a chapel to the glory of God, should he ever be released. At the Restoration (1660) he was released and returned to his academic posts in Cambridge, where he commissioned a young architect, his nephew, Christopher Wren, to design and build a chapel for Pembroke. This chapel, Wren's first important building, abuts the pavement of Trumpington Street. It was a kind of template for the great Church of St Paul's which he was later to build in the City of London after the Great Fire (1666). If you have time, go into the college through the Porter's Lodge, turn right and enter the chapel. It's well worth a visit.

Across the road from Pembroke, on the right side, is the 18th century Kenmare House, set back from the road, and Emmanuel United Reform Church, a rather ugly building built in 1874, with its tower sitting uncomfortably on indifferently coloured brickwork and which might be called "hideo-colossal", a term coined by an architectural student some years ago.

A cupola graces the top of Pembroke College's Chapel. It would have been used as a lantern in the two centuries following its completion in 1665.

Palladian, or Venetian,   *G* windows grace the front of Kenmare House. The classic tripartite window we see here dates to the mid-18th century.

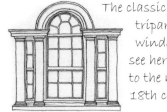

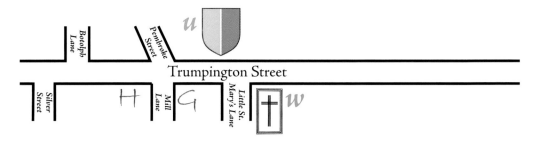

Little St Mary's Lane

Little St Mary's Lane

Still on the right hand side of Trumpington Street, there runs a narrow medieval lane of small houses, they originally housed the bargees who brought corn and coal along the river to the Mill pool. These houses formed the western side of the King's Ditch boundary of Cambridge. The King's Ditch ran from the river Cam near Magdalene College across central Cambridge, down Pembroke Street and then finally back to the Cam. Built mainly by Henry III, it made taking tolls from travelling traders easier as it made them pass through the gates to get to the markets.
On the other side of this lane is Little St Mary's Church.

H

A turreted tower and a small entrance porch abut the main church building. The position of the twisting staircase is indicated by the alignment of the middle windows.

Little St Mary's Church   *w*

"St Mary the Less" as opposed to Great St Mary's church which you walked past in the town centre.
This is a 12th century building, historically interesting in that, just inside beyond the Norman doorway is a tablet in memory of the Reverend George Washington (1670-1729), a Fellow of nearby Peterhouse, and

ancestor of the George Washington, who led the American colonists in their rebellion against the mother country, and became the first President of the United States of America. The Washington armorial bearings, showing the 'stars and stripes', erected here in 1736, were in 1776 incorporated into the flag and crest of the USA.

Section Eleven - Peterhouse   *x*

The University had its origins in a dispute between 'town and gown' in Oxford. In 1209 a group of Oxford scholars moved to Cambridge and established a new seat of learning in a pre-existing school here. This makes Cambridge the fourth oldest university in the world after Bologna, Paris and Oxford. In 1280 the first college, Peterhouse, was formed. It originally occupied a site within St. John's Hospital, at the northern end of the High Street, where St John's College now stands. In 1284 the Bishop of Ely, Hugh de Balsham, founded Peterhouse at its present site, here beside St Mary the Less. The bishop built it to provide safe lodgings for students at the University, some of whom were as young as fourteen and at risk

The range of buildings that house the Porters' Lodge at Peterhouse date back to the Early Middle Ages, but apart from the 17th century oriel window in the street-side gable end, practically all the other details were restored in the 19th. Here we have a pair of angled chimney clusters, dormer windows of gothick design, and battlements.

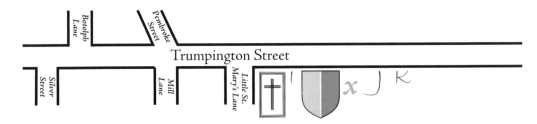

Peterhouse Chapel was completed in 1633 as a new building in a medieval setting. It was linked to the older buildings by the raised galleries over walkways that we see today. This casement window with

its small pieces of glass, called quarries, and its narrow lead-wrapped iron frames, known as calms (pronounced 'cames') dates to this time.

Gray's window

living in lodgings in town. Students studied mainly Theology, Grammar, Latin and Mathematics and were destined for the church, which employed all educated, literate men.

Peterhouse chapel, set well back from the road, was begun in 1628 and is one of the rare church buildings created between the Reformation and the Restoration. The tall building to the right of the chapel is the Burrough's Building, where the poet, Thomas Gray (1716–1761) best known as the author of 'Elegy in a Country Churchyard', had rooms on the second floor. Gray was a hypochondriac and fearful of all things. He particularly worried that the boisterous, often drunken, students on the floors below would set the place on fire, and requested the college to put a safety bar across his window to which he could attach a rope ladder, should he need to make a quick escape. If you look up at that room on the side of the building next to Little St Mary's you will see the bar still there.

One night, when the downstairs occupants had got wind of Gray's scheme, they put a bath of cold water at the point where his rope ladder would reach the ground and in the early hours of the next morning began to shout 'Fire, Fire', woke Gray, who rushed to his bedroom window, hooked his rope ladder to the bar, and beginning to climb out, saw the giggling recalcitrants on the ground floor and realised it was a hoax.

The next day, Gray arranged to move across the road and became a Fellow of Pembroke College!

Section Twelve - Trumpington Street III

Peterhouse Master's Lodge *y*

Back on the left side of Trumpington Street is Peterhouse Master's Lodge. All heads of college in Cambridge have varying titles – President, Provost, Warden, Principal, Mistress – but the majority use the title Master. All the colleges are independent institutions, quite separate from the university, with their own statutes and financial structures. They were originally founded as living quarters for undergraduates of the university, which provided the educational courses. The nature of medieval colleges is maintained in the name of this first Cambridge college i.e. Peterhouse, not Peterhouse College.

The Peterhouse Master's Lodge

Peterhouse Master's Lodge is unique in that a college's Master's Lodge was normally built as an integral part of the college. This one, however, is on the opposite side of the road to Peterhouse and was built four hundred years after the college's foundation, in 1702, by one of its Fellows, Dr. Charles Beaumont, son of a former Master, Joseph Beaumont. In his will Charles Beaumont bequeathed the house to the college as a Master's Lodge, which function it has served ever since his death in 1727. Its beautifully proportioned front of delicate red brick makes it unquestionably

This beautifully proportioned building is a superb example of an early 18th century town house. The quality of the wood and workmanship demonstrated in this principal door and its surrounds is supreme. Such a sophisticated façade puts this house in the category of 'polite architecture'.

L

Trumpington Street

Fitzwilliam Street

L y z M N L

Little St. Mary's Lane

one of the finest eighteenth century houses in Cambridge. The Fellows of a college are the senior academic members of the college, who, under the Master, who is himself elected by the Fellows, form the college's governing body, usually called the college council. This is a self-perpetuating body, new Fellows being chosen by the existing Fellows. Democracy is maintained by junior members of the college having their own councils, who act as advisers to the Fellows.

The Hostel

The Hostel z

Standing next to the Peterhouse Master's Lodge, this hostel was built in 1926 to house members of Peterhouse and their guests.

The next range of 17th, 18th and 19th century buildings originally formed part of the faubourg outside the Trumpington Gate entrance to the town by the King's Ditch, and terminates in Fitzwilliam House, now belonging to Cambridge University.

This Newsagent's Shop has very significant details that show the many alterations and remodelling that have created changes M

in the building's appearance over 300 years or more. This house is categorised as 'vernacular architecture'.

17th century buildings before Fitzwilliam House

Section Thirteen - Trumpington Street IV

Fitzwilliam House   *A*

This was built in 1727 as a private house by John Halstead. In 1869 it became a lodging house for undergraduates who did not belong to a college, but its members from 1874 counted as a collegiate community, although not a statutory college. They adopted the name of Fitzwilliam House in 1920 from the name of the museum opposite. In 1960, they moved to newly-built premises in Huntingdon Road, on the northern edge of the city and in 1966 were granted full collegiate status, as Fitzwilliam College. The building is now used to house various University administrative offices and faculty rooms.

The 18th century town house is older than its name which it took from the museum opposite. This sash window has retained its original 1720 appearance, its projecting brick apron was an expensive fashionable detail of its day.

The Fitzwilliam Museum   *B*

Across the road is the magnificent 19th century baroque building, begun in the first year of Victoria's reign, 1837, from a design by George Basevi, who was also surveyor to Ely Cathedral and had the misfortune in 1845 to fall through the belfry of the west tower to his untimely death. The work of completing the building was assumed by Charles Cockerill, a London architect, who was professor of Architecture to the Royal Academy and designed the 1840 Cambridge University Library as well as the Taylorean Building in Oxford.

Fitzwilliam Museum fresco

The Fitzwilliam Museum

Q   *A* Fitzwilliam Street ○   Lensfield Road

Trumpington Street

B   P

The earliest part of the Fitzwilliam Museum building was completed by 1850 and can be discovered by observing the symmetrical pattern extending from the central portico and its columns. The musician can be found playing her lyre in the lofty position next to the winged angel.

The building of the Museum was funded by a bequest of £100,000 from Viscount Fitzwilliam of Merrion, who, on his Grand Tour through Europe after leaving his Cambridge college, Trinity Hall, had amassed a large collection of paintings, books, prints, manuscripts and objets d'art, which he wanted to donate to his old university and display in suitably grand surroundings. The site was acquired from Peterhouse in 1823 but did not become fully available until 1840. It took until 1871 to finish the building, as funds ran out after Basevi's death and new money had to be found. There have been a number of extensions to the building, the latest being in 2003-4.

The Fitzwilliam is one of the most eminent museums and art galleries outside London and has been called 'the finest small museum in Europe'. It should be one of your priorities for a visit if you have an hour or two to spare, take note though it is closed on Mondays.

The museum also has a café situated in the covered courtyard, great for a morning coffee or afternoon tea.

The Fitzwilliam
Museum extension

The central window's position so much higher than its neighbours suggests that, at an earlier time, the waggon entrance was taller to permit entry for higher loads. The small dwellings up in the yard indicate changes of use from agricultural to craft trades in the 19th century.

Section Fourteen - Trumpington Street V

The Judge Institute C

This Institute of Management Studies, back on the left side of Trumpington Street, is the latest addition to Cambridge University's academic departments. Before it was established in 1990, Cambridge did not consider Business and Management Studies worthy of a place in any self-respecting University's programme of studies. It has become in a very short time a world-renowned institute to equal the Harvard Business School.

The Judge Institute

Paul and Anne Judge provided the funds for the conversion of Old Addenbrooke's Hospital, first established here in 1766 and extended throughout the first half of the 19th century and again in 1915 and 1930, and incorporated elements of the hospital into the design of their foundation. The hospital moved to its new site on the southern edge of Cambridge in 1984 and the Judge Institute moved into the refurbished building in 1995.

R

Best viewed from the museum side of the street – so mind the traffic – the explanation of this small house's chimney stack becomes evident. Its survival as a house amidst all the surrounding development is because it must have been privately owned and not available for sale long enough for the authorities in 1973 to list it as a monument.

C T   R   S   W   Lensfield Road

Trumpington Street

The Judge Institute - detail

Designed by John Outram, a British design architect noted for his provocative use of interior and exterior decoration, it is a glorious example of late 20th century colour and design. Regrettably it is not open to the general public, so its ingenious adaptations of the corridors and wards within can be seen only by its own members. Originally the Institute was designed to have an innovative roof garden, actually only half way up the building, but this plan was scrapped late in the day.

Next to the Judge Institute is Brown's restaurant, occupying what once was a clinic in Addenbrooke's Hospital. On the pavement outside is one of the famous red K6 'Jubilee' telephone boxes. Designed by Sir Giles Gilbert Scott to commemorate the Silver Jubilee of King George V in 1935.

S   This is the pattern of the window sill guards along the first floor of 25-27 Trumpington Street. The arabesque lines and the floral motifs are based upon the honeysuckle, the Anthemion. The linear wave theme is called a Vitruvian scroll

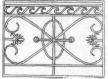

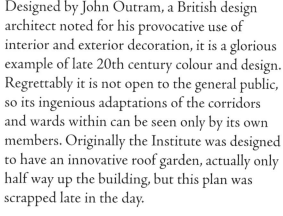

No.10 Trumpington Street has this rare survival from the early 20th century, possibly 1905. It is a cast-iron stepped-porch with a ramped and flared zinc roof. They don't come much grander than that.

Section Fifteen - the final footsteps   D

Hobson's fountain.

Across from Lensfield Road, on a corner beside a stream, stands Hobson's Fountain. Between 1614 and 1856 this Jacobean fountain stood on Market Hill, in the center of Cambridge. Thomas Hobson, a Cambridge carrier in the late sixteenth century, diverted water from a stream rising in Nine Wells, just south of Cambridge, into a culvert which ran along Trumpington Street up to his stables near St. Catharine's College, and then along roadside channels into the market place where he erected this fountain. The fountain was moved to this site after Cambridge got a piped water supply in the mid 19th century.

He provided this amenity for all the many working horses that abounded in Cambridge at this time, as well as his own. You can still see Hobson's conduit running along each side of Trumpington Street, they have been listed as architectural monuments and cannot be covered over, or interfered with in any way, much to the chagrin of modern motorists and planners who would like to see them disappear under tarmac, so that the road could be widened.

Hobson's fountain

Scroope Terrace and the Royal Cambridge Hotel make up a stylish 19th century terrace with fine looking windows and doors. The small drawing depicts the one surviving chimney stack from the early 19th century. This was the fashionable shape for covering chimneys prior to the creation of chimney-pots in the second half of that century.

u

V   Lensfield Road   D

Trumpington Street

u

On the opposite side of the Trumpington Street-Lensfield Road corner to Hobson's Conduit Head stands the oldest surviving house at this southern end of our walk. Like so many houses of some antiquity it has been much altered throughout the centuries, with considerable additions during the 1930s and later in the '50s. This is 'The Corner House'.

Here we end our walk, we hope you have enjoyed this historic stroll. During the route, you have just completed, you have passed through a thousand years of English history and walked in the footsteps of the Roman Legions who marched along this way a thousand years before that. Vale! - farewell.

Many thanks go to Marilyn Barnes and Sophie Barnes for their scrupulous attention to detail on subbing the text and to Rachel, Chloe and Evie Barnes for their support whilst producing this guide. Thanks also to Michael Wood for all his help with the revised edition.

Scientists at Cambridge University

Charles Babbage - invented first 'computer' in 1814.
Henry Cavendish - discovered hydrogen "inflammable air" in 1766
Subrahmanyan Chandrasekhar - discovered the behaviour of collapsing stars in 1935.
Francis Crick and James Watson - discovered the structure of DNA in 1953.
Charles Darwin - described the mechanism of evolution in 1859.
William Harvey - discovered the circulation of the blood in 1628.
Stephen Hawking - mathematician, wrote A Brief History of Time in 1988.
James Clerk Maxwell - did revolutionary work in electromagnetism 1873
Isaac Newton - published Principia Mathematica in 1687, discovered gravity.
Ernest Rutherford -nuclear physicist who won the Nobel Prize in Chemistry in 1908

Writers and Thinkers at Cambridge University

Douglas Adams, 1952-2001. St John's College.
Francis Bacon, 1561-1626. Trinity College.
A S Byatt, 1936. Newnham College.
E M Forster, 1879-1970. King's College.
C S Lewis, 1898-1963. Magdalene College.
Christopher Marlowe, 1564-1593. Corpus Christi College.
Vladimir Nabokov, 1899-1977. Trinity College.
A A Milne, 1882-1956. Trinity College.
Samuel Pepys, 1633-1703. Magdalene College.
Bertrand Russell, 1872-1970. Trinity College
William Thackeray, 1811-1868. Trinity College.

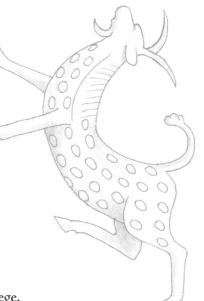

Poets at Cambridge University

Rupert Brooke, 1887-1915. King's College.
Lord Byron 1788-1824. Trinity College.
Samuel Coleridge, 1772-1834. Jesus College.
John Dryden, 1631-1700. Trinity College.
Thomas Gray, 1716-1771. Pembroke College.
A E Housman, 1859-1936. Trinity College.
Ted Hughes, 1930 - 1998. Pembroke College.
John Milton, 1608-1674. Christ's College.
Sylvia Plath, 1932-1963. Newnham College.
Siegfried Sassoon, 1886-1967. Clare College.
Alfred Tennyson, 1809-1892. Trinity College.
William Wordsworth, 1770-1850. St John's College.

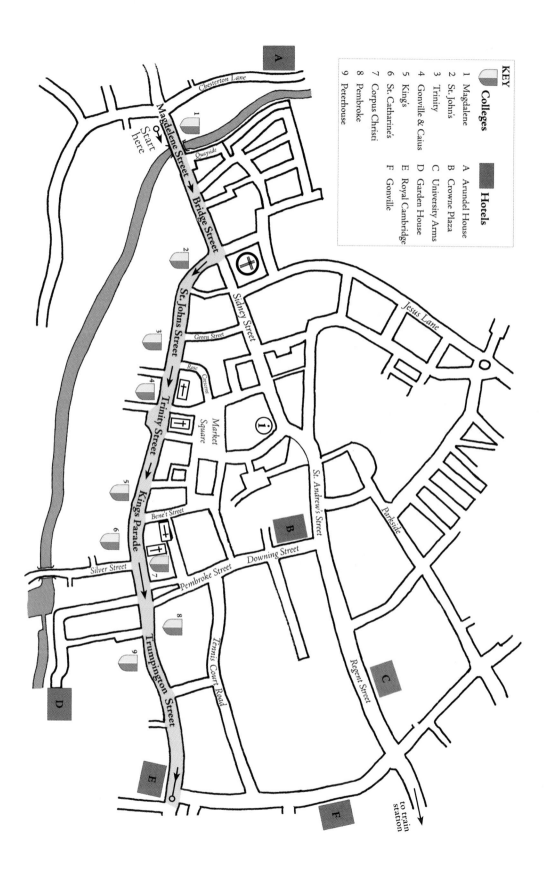

Cambridge
City for all seasons

The aim of this guide is simple - to make your
visit to Cambridge enjoyable and informative.

Easy to read and easy to follow, the Shortcut Through
Time Guide helps you explore a thousand years of Cambridge's
history at your own pace. Written by local author Roy Barnes
and with illustrations and insights by the famous architectural
historian Mac Dowdy this guide takes you along the
historic 'main mile' on an informative walk.

With a city map in the back and split into easy-to-walk
sections, the 'shortcut through time' will transport you back
to the Middle Ages, the time of knights and kings, on through
Newton and Darwin to the architecture of the 21st century.
You can even visit the same pub as the famous scientists,
Crick and Watson, who discovered the structure of
DNA here in Cambridge in 1953.

Resident, student or visitor, if you are interested in this
beautiful city around you, take the 'shortcut through time.'™

Pedibus ambulans animo percipe - walk and learn.

Cambridgeshire Association for Local History
Book Award 2007

shortcutpublishing.co.uk
UK £4.99

ISBN 978-0-9556086-0-5

9 780955 608605